Blessed Teresa of Calcutta

Missionary of Charity

Written by
Mary Kathleen Glavich, SND

Illustrated by
Barbara Kiwak

auline
BOOKS & MEDIA
Boston

Library of Congress Cataloging-in-Publication Data

Glavich, Mary Kathleen.
  Blessed Teresa of Calcutta : missionary of charity / written by
Mary Kathleen Glavich ; illustrated by Barbara Kiwak.
     p. cm. — (Encounter the saints series ; 17)
Summary: Profiles Mother Teresa of Calcutta, the Yugoslavian nun
who became a missionary to India, dedicated her life to serving
the poorest of the poor, and founded the Missionaries of Charity,
a congregation of Roman Catholic sisters who carry on her work.
  ISBN 0-8198-1160-2 (pbk.)
  1. Teresa, Mother, 1910—Juvenile literature. 2. Missionaries
of Charity—Biography—Juvenile literature. [1. Teresa, Mother,
1910– 2. Missionaries of Charity. 3. Missionaries. 4. Nuns.
5. Women—Biography. 6. Nobel prizes—Biography.] I. Kiwak,
Barbara, ill. II. Title. III. Series.
  BX4406.5.Z8G57 2003
  271'.97—dc22

                                      2003015042

"P" and PAULINE are registered trademarks of the Daughters of
St. Paul.

Text copyright © 2003, Sr. Mary Kathleen Glavich, SND
Edition copyright © 2003, Daughters of St. Paul

Published by Pauline Books & Media, 50 Saint Pauls Avenue,
Boston, MA 02130-3491.

Printed in the U.S.A.

www.pauline.org

Pauline Books & Media is the publishing house of the Daughters
of St. Paul, an international congregation of women religious
serving the Church with the communications media.

3 4 5 6 7 8 9 10   12 11 10 09 08 07 06

Encounter the Saints Series

Blesseds Jacinta and Francisco Marto
Shepherds of Fatima

Blessed Pier Giorgio Frassati
Journey to the Summit

Blessed Teresa of Calcutta
Missionary of Charity

Journeys with Mary
Apparitions of Our Lady

Saint Anthony of Padua
Fire and Light

Saint Bakhita of Sudan
Forever Free

Saint Bernadette Soubirous
Light in the Grotto

Saint Edith Stein
Blessed by the Cross

Saint Elizabeth Ann Seton
Daughter of America

Saint Frances Xavier Cabrini
Cecchina's Dream

Saint Francis of Assisi
Gentle Revolutionary

Saint Ignatius of Loyola
For the Greater Glory of God

Saint Isaac Jogues
With Burning Heart

Saint Joan of Arc
God's Soldier

Saint Juan Diego
And Our Lady of Guadalupe

Saint Julie Billiart
The Smiling Saint

Saint Katharine Drexel
The Total Gift

Saint Martin de Porres
Humble Healer

Saint Maximilian Kolbe
Mary's Knight

Saint Pio of Pietrelcina
Rich in Love

Saint Thérèse of Lisieux
The Way of Love

For other children's titles on the Saints,
visit our Web site: www.pauline.org

Contents

1

HAPPY YEARS

"I don't know how your little one can sleep through this noise!" Sara remarked to her friend Drana as the two women arranged pastries on a platter.

"It seems my Agnes can sleep through anything," Drana Bojaxhiu laughed. She had put the two-year-old to bed as their large house began to fill with visitors. Lazar, her four-year-old son and Aga, who was eight, were allowed to stay up later than usual for the occasion. "It isn't every night that we can celebrate our country's independence," Mrs Bojaxhiu explained to them.

The year was 1912, and Albania, the native country of Drana and her husband Nicholas, had finally won independence from Serbia. The family's home in the nearby city of Skopje, Yugoslavia (today part of the Republic of Macedonia) had often been a meeting place for Albanian rebels. Mr. Bojaxhiu also supported them financially.

"Did you notice, Drana? Even our best fighter Curri is here. Imagine how he feels today," Sara mused.

"I don't have to imagine," said Drana. "Just listen."

The sounds of laughter, singing, and the mandolin poured into the kitchen. Lazar burst into the room. "Mom," he called excitedly, "they've built a fire!"

The women rushed to see. The jubilant men had gathered matchboxes in the center of the room. A blazing fire reached to the ceiling, a symbol of their triumph and joy. The victory party lasted all night. Nicholas Bojaxhiu had seen his dream of a free Albania fulfilled.

Mrs. Bojaxhiu went to check on Agnes and found her still asleep. "Gonxha," she whispered, using the family nickname, "so pink and plump, you are just what your name means, a rosebud." The mother gently pushed dark tendrils away from the girl's forehead and kissed it. "You have a very happy father today," she said. Drana, married at sixteen to thirty-four-year-old Nicholas, called Kole for short, was deeply in love with her husband.

Kole had more interests than politics. He was in turn business assistant to a pharmacist, a building contractor, and finally a merchant. Knowing several languages helped make him a success in the marketplace. Business trips to other countries often took him away from home.

When Agnes was five, she and her brother and sister were sitting with their mother one evening, talking.

"Mom, when is Dad coming home?" Agnes asked. "I miss him."

Mrs. Bojaxhiu sighed. "We all do," she answered. "I expect him sometime this week."

"Good!" said Lazar. "He always brings great gifts. Who knows what he'll find for us in Egypt!"

"Lazar, is that why you want Father home—for his gifts?" teased Aga.

"Of course not!" Lazar shook his head vigorously. "But you know you like his gifts as much as I do."

"What I like even *better* are his stories," Aga retorted.

"Yes," Mrs. Bojaxhiu smiled, "your father always manages to have adventures and meet the most interesting people."

"Listen," said Agnes. "Someone's coming." Suddenly the door swung open and in strode Mr. Bojaxhiu, his arms laden with packages. "Dad!" the three children cried as they rushed toward him. Mrs. Bojaxhiu smiled as she helped her husband set the packages down. He embraced her and then hugged each child in turn.

"Aga, how's my right hand? Have you been a help to your mom?" Mr. Bojaxhiu asked.

"I tried, Dad," Aga said.

"She's been a great help, Kole," assured Mrs. Bojaxhiu. "They've all been good."

"I would hope so," Mr. Bojaxhiu went on, wagging a finger and trying to look serious. "Like I always say, 'Never forget whose children you are!'"

"Lazar!" boomed Mr. Bojaxhiu, clapping his son on the shoulder, "I think you've grown another inch."

He turned and picked up Agnes. "And you, Gonxha—you look a tad pale. How do you feel?"

"I've been sick again, Papa," Agnes admitted.

"Yes, Kole, she had the whooping cough," Mrs. Bojaxhiu explained.

"Well, we'll just have to make you stronger, now won't we," Mr. Bojaxhiu said, giving his youngest a kiss on the cheek.

"Before I forget, Drana," he went on, "I met the new priest on my way home and invited him to dinner tomorrow. I hope that's all right."

"Of course, Kole. We always have room for one more," his wife replied. She was used to hosting archbishops, politicians, and strangers.

"What about that old woman?" Mr. Bojaxhiu asked. "Has she been coming to dinner? And have you all welcomed her with love?" Mr. Bojaxhiu looked around at his children.

"Yes, Father." Three heads bobbed up and down.

"That's good." Mr. Bojaxhiu looked pleased.

"Now, children, let your father unpack and freshen up," Mrs. Bojaxhiu instructed. "You can open your presents and listen to his stories after evening prayers."

"Yes. Wait until you hear what happened to me on this trip!" Mr. Bojaxhiu rolled his eyes. His family laughed. "I'll tell you all about it later. I also want to hear what you've been learning at school. I'm not sending all three of you to Sacred Heart's for nothing."

Mr. Bojaxhiu looked over the children's heads at his wife. "It's good to be home again," he sighed.

But such happy homecomings were soon to end....

2

FAMILY OF LOVE

Tragedy struck the Bojaxhiu family in 1917, when Agnes was seven. One day, Mr. Bojaxhiu was at a meeting in Belgrade with other city councilors. In the early evening there was a knock at the Bojaxhiu door. Drana opened it a crack and saw a strange man holding his hat in his hands. "Mrs. Bojaxhiu," he began, "I'm sorry, but your husband is very ill. Some of us think he's been poisoned. We brought him home in the Italian consul's carriage."

The blood drained from Mrs. Bojaxhiu's face. "Would you please take him right to the hospital?" she asked. "Wait. I'll get my shawl." She turned to her three children standing wide-eyed behind her. "Aga," she directed, "take care of your brother and sister. Let Sara know that I've gone to the hospital." Hastily kissing them, she left with the man.

The next day Mr. Bojaxhiu underwent surgery. The following day he died.

Hundreds of people came to the funeral to honor Mr. Bojaxhiu. Among other things, he was responsible for having built their town's first theater. On the day he was buried, stores closed. It was the custom for students to receive handkerchiefs as mementos of the death of a public figure. The number distributed depended on the deceased person's importance. In the case of Mr. Bojaxhiu, all students in every school received a handkerchief.

After the funeral services, Mrs. Bojaxhiu went to her room. For several months, she lay in a kind of trance, grieving. She finally recovered and was determined to support her family. One night at dinner she made an announcement. "Children, up until now we've been very well provided for by your father's business. His partner, though, says he will no longer be associated with us. We'll just have to be more careful with our money from now on."

"Will that mean we won't have enough money for food?" Lazar asked in an anxious voice.

"No, Lazar. Don't worry," Mrs. Bojaxhiu reassured him. "We won't be holding large parties like we used to, but we certainly won't starve. I have a plan. Your mother is quite a seamstress, you know. I will begin a business sewing fine clothes for ladies."

"Like wedding dresses and costumes for our festivals?" asked Agnes.

"Yes," smiled Mrs. Bojaxhiu.

"But, Mom, do you have to work?" Lazar broke in. "Doesn't your family own some large estates? The parish priest has asked me several times why you don't ask for your share."

Mrs. Bojaxhiu shook her head. "There's disagreement about who owns those lands," she explained. "Unfortunately, I have no documents to prove my claim to them. That's all right. I enjoy sewing. Really." She leaned over and ruffled Lazar's hair.

"There are other ways of being rich anyway," Agnes observed. She was beginning to resemble her mother more and more, not only in her physical appearance but also in her values.

When the children were older, they attended public schools, but Mrs. Bojaxhiu and the local parish made sure that they were well grounded in their Catholic faith. Perhaps because Catholics were a small minority in their country, parish feasts and celebrations were many and well attended.

In addition to going to Mass every day, the Bojaxhiu family made a pilgrimage each year in their horse-drawn carriage to the Madonna of Letnice. The popular shrine was in the mountains. The family stayed in a house that Mr. Bojaxhiu had helped a friend build.

One day while Agnes and Lazar were outside playing under the fruit trees in their spacious garden at Skopje, Mrs. Bojaxhiu and Aga were alone. "I'm concerned about Gonxha," Mrs. Bojaxhiu admitted. "We go to the hot springs every year for our vacation, hoping she'll get stronger, but she's still not healthy. This year maybe you two could go to Letnice a few weeks early. Some extra rest and sunshine would be good for Gonxha. What do you think?"

"I'd love to go early!" Aga exclaimed. "We all enjoy being there. To spend extra days will be wonderful, especially if it will help Gonxha."

"Now you must make sure that she doesn't spend all the time with her nose in a book," her mother cautioned. "You know how she sits for hours in the church library here. It's fresh air and exercise that she needs."

"I'll see that she walks every day, Mom," Aga promised.

"I trust you, Aga. You're a responsible girl," Mrs. Bojaxhiu said, giving her older daughter a quick hug.

Aga kept her word. Each day the two sisters could be seen walking the streets of Letnice together. As Aga and Agnes strolled, they talked about everything, including their family.

"Aga, we're lucky to have such good parents, aren't we?" Agnes said.

"Yes, Gonxha. Father always seemed strict, but he had a big heart for the poor. Remember how often he sent Lazar out with food, money, and other things for the poor?"

"You know, Aga," Agnes replied, "when I was little I used to think that all the guests around our table were relatives. Instead they turned out to be people who just needed a decent meal. Father once said to me, 'Daughter, never take a morsel of food that you are not prepared to share with others.'"

"And Mother's a good match for him," Aga said. "Whenever someone needs help, she's always right there."

"She teaches us by her example," Agnes replied thoughtfully. "When I go with her to bring food to that widow whose son left her, I help clean the house. To be honest, it makes me feel good. I guess we could have ended up spoiled if our parents weren't so holy," she laughed.

"Not many children from well-to-do families like ours have chores like cleaning the family shoes every night the way we do," Aga pointed out. "By the way, I noticed that Lazar usually talks you into taking his turn at the shoes." The two girls had reached the end of the street. They turned and headed back to the house.

"I wonder how Lazar will turn out," Aga continued. "Mom's always telling him to be more like you, even though you're younger than he is."

"I know," Agnes chuckled. "I never told Mom how Lazar sneaks into the kitchen at night for jam and sweets. Poor Lazar! Remember how Father used to wake him up at night to quiz him on school subjects?"

"Yes," Aga said. "Thank goodness it's not so necessary that girls be educated!"

"Well, I'm glad I go to school," admitted Agnes. "I've always dreamed of being a teacher someday. At times I think I might want to write or do something with music."

"You'll be good at whatever you do, Gonxha," Aga predicted. "C'mon. I'll race you home!"

When the family returned to Skopje, Mrs. Bojaxhiu began to care for File, an alcoholic who was ill and covered with sores. Twice a day Mrs. Bojaxhiu went to wash the woman and take care of her needs. Agnes accompanied her. On the way Agnes once remarked, "Mother, everyone must think you're a saint!" Mrs. Bojaxhiu looked at her daughter in surprise. "The point to doing good is not to have people think well of you. When you do good, do it without show, as if you were tossing a pebble into the sea."

One evening as Mrs. Bojaxhiu and her children were sitting by the fireplace, she confided, "I'm so blessed that I have the health to care for you. A widow I visit isn't as lucky. I'm afraid she will die soon, and her six children will be left orphans. What would you think about having them come live with us as part of our family?"

After a brief silence, Aga spoke up. "Why not?"

"It would be exciting to have more brothers and sisters!" Agnes added.

"Dad would like that," Lazar agreed.

And so the family grew.

Years later, Agnes was to comment, "We were a family full of joy and love, and we children were happy and contented."

In spite of this, Agnes would choose to leave home at an early age.

3

MISSION CALL

When Agnes was eleven years old, the Jesuits took over her parish, Sacred Heart Church. The new pastor was a blessing for the community in many ways. One day Agnes said to Lazar, "I feel that you don't much like Father Zadrima."

"How can I like him," Lazar replied, "when he's always walking around with that huge stick?" (To ensure good behavior in church the priest carried a big stick—but never used it.)

"Still," Agnes reminded her older brother, "it's your duty to love him and respect him. He is Christ's priest."

Then an assistant priest who could hardly speak Albanian came to Sacred Heart's. Agnes became his interpreter for religion classes and joined in the activities he held for youth.

In 1924 the dynamic Father Jambrenkovic was appointed pastor of the parish. He started a Sodality of the Sisters of Mary (a society for girls) and organized a youth group. Agnes was active in everything. She and Aga were in the church choir and sometimes sang duets. Agnes had a lovely soprano voice, while Aga sang contralto. People said, "They are our church's two nightingales."

One day in 1924 Mrs. Bojaxhiu and her friend Sara were talking in the garden.

"You must be very proud of Agnes," Sara said. "She's always at the top of her class. She can act, sing, play the accordion and the mandolin, write poetry, and is a born leader."

"I'm proud of all my children," Drana replied. "Aga is doing well studying economics in college. Lazar won that scholarship to study for a year in Austria. He'll be coming home soon. But you're right. Agnes is special. She always surprises me. She's so frail and slight, yet so gifted." Mrs. Bojaxhiu's expression grew serious. "Sometimes I think she will not be with me for long," she confided. "Either I'll lose her because of her poor health, or she'll give herself to God as a sister."

"Did Agnes ever tell you she wanted to be a sister?" Sara asked.

"When she was twelve," Drana replied. "I told her to put it out of her mind. She was only a child."

Mrs. Bojaxhiu's thoughts were prophetic. Unknowingly, she herself was fostering Agnes's religious vocation by praying with her in church and saying the rosary at home. The new pastor also was planting seeds that would take Agnes far from home.

Father Jambrenkovic had a heart for the missions. He prayed for them, took up collections for them, and gave sermons and talks about them. Among the Catholic newspapers and magazines that Father passed out at church was *Catholic Missions.* It contained reports from local Yugoslav missionaries working in Calcutta, India. These fascinated Agnes.

One day a Jesuit missionary from India visited Skopje and spoke in the parish church. Agnes's large brown eyes glowed as she listened to his stories. He unrolled a large map showing the locations of various Catholic missions. Afterwards, Agnes asked some very good questions and shared some of what she knew about the missions. A woman in the audience whispered to her neighbor, "Young Agnes Bojaxhiu has become an expert on the missions, hasn't she?"

Agnes thought and prayed about becoming a sister. She pondered the words of one missionary: "Each person has a special road to follow, and one must follow that road." Lazar came home for a year and then left for the Military Academy of Tirana in Albania. He was following his own road. As Agnes struggled to learn whether or not she had a vocation to religious life, she consulted her mother. This time Drana encouraged her, saying, "My daughter, if you begin something, begin it wholeheartedly. Otherwise, don't begin it at all. Go with my blessing. But strive to live only and all for God and for Jesus Christ."

Agnes turned to her confessor for advice. She asked, "How can I know if God is really calling me, and if so, *what* God is calling me to?"

"You will know by your feelings," the wise priest answered. "If the thought of being a sister and serving God and people makes you happy, then your vocation is genuine. A deep inner joy is like a compass that points you in the direction God wants you to go. This is true even if the road for you is difficult."

The road to becoming a missionary sister did look difficult. Agnes was very close to her mother. She would have to leave her as well as Aga and Lazar. She would have to part from her friends and relatives. She would have to leave her country and perhaps even sacrifice her dream of being a teacher.

After she turned sixteen, Agnes spent a total of two months praying at the shrine of the Madonna of Letnice. She also made several retreats. By the time she was eighteen, Agnes was convinced that God was calling her to be a sister and serve the poor as a missionary. She never doubted her vocation after that.

When Agnes broke the news to her mother, Mrs. Bojaxhiu went to her room and stayed there for a full twenty-four hours. When she finally came out, she said, "Gonxha, put your hand in God's and walk all the way with him."

And that's just what Agnes did.

4

LEAVING HOME

Because Agnes wanted to go to India, she applied to the congregation of the Sisters of Loreto, which had missionaries there. Agnes would have to travel to the sisters' motherhouse in Ireland to enter the community. She would also have to learn English before being sent to India.

After she had mailed in her application to the community, Agnes wrote to Lazar, who had enlisted in the Albanian army. He responded immediately to her news. "How can a girl like you do such a thing?" he wrote. "Do you realize what you're doing—sacrificing yourself for the rest of your life, burying yourself alive in the middle of nowhere?"

Agnes calmly wrote back, "You think you are important because you are an officer serving a king with two million subjects. But I am serving the King of the whole world. Which of us do you think is in the better place?" This response changed Lazar's attitude.

On August 15, 1928, the Feast of the Assumption, Agnes visited the shrine at Letnice for the last time and prayed to the Madonna. Then she returned home to prepare for her departure on September 26.

The night before Agnes was to leave, friends from her parish and school gathered at her home. Each one brought a gift and thanked Agnes for the gift she was to them. Lorenz Antoni, a composer who had fostered Agnes's musical talents, presented her with a gold fountain pen. "A reminder to write us," he explained.

A friend warned, "Agnes, we'll all be at the train station tomorrow to wave you off."

"Better bring plenty of handkerchiefs!" someone else called out.

Agnes smiled. "I won't cry," she replied. "I'll be too excited and happy."

At the train station the next day Mr. Antoni bought tickets for Mrs. Bojaxhiu, Aga, and Agnes. The three would travel to Zagreb together. Mr. Antoni made his way though the friends and relatives crowding around Agnes. Everyone was crying—*even* Agnes. "There must be a hundred people here!" the composer remarked to Mrs. Bojaxhiu as he handed her the tickets.

Everyone was crying—even Agnes.

Soon it was time to board the train. Her friends could see Agnes from the platform. As the train moved away, they waved handkerchiefs. Agnes waved back until she could no longer be seen.

I wonder what will become of this girl leaving for India, a strange land so far away, Mr. Antoni thought.

The *Catholic Mission* reported Agnes's departure: "Just as St. Peter immediately left his nets behind him, so Gonxha left her books and set off in the name of God. Everyone was surprised, because she was top of her class and much admired. She was the life and soul of the Catholic girls' activities and church choir, and it was generally acknowledged that her departure would leave an enormous gap."

The Bojaxhius stayed in Zagreb almost three weeks so that Agnes could meet up with another girl, Betika, who was also joining the Loreto Sisters. Together the two would take the long train ride through Austria, Switzerland and France. They would cross the channel, travel to London, and then sail on to Ireland.

Betika arrived. Agnes said a final goodbye to her mother and sister and boarded the train. She didn't know it then, but she would never see them again. Since Agnes's birth in August of 1910, her mother had been the guiding force in her life.

Now Agnes was on her own.

5

A LORETO SISTER

As their boat docked in Dublin, Agnes stood on the deck. "Look, Betika!" she exclaimed, pointing at the crowd on the shore. "There are the sisters!" The Mother Superior and two other Loreto sisters had come to meet them. The sisters were easy to spot in their long black habits and veils.

Before long Agnes and Betika were welcomed by all the sisters at Loreto Abbey, where they joined the other postulants. Mother Borgia Irwin saw to it that her students were immersed in English, which was to be their spoken language. In addition, the postulants began to learn what it meant to be a sister and live in a community.

For barely two months Agnes called the Abbey home. Then on December 1, 1928, she and Betika boarded the ship, *The Marcha*, and set sail for India. It would be seven weeks before they arrived in Darjeeling, where the novitiate house of the Sisters of Loreto awaited them. The ocean voyage was rough and tiring. Except for three Franciscan sisters, the girls were the only Catholics on the ship.

Alone in their small cabin on Christmas Eve, Agnes and Betika discussed their situation.

"I wish there were a priest on board," Betika sighed. "It's hard enough not having Mass for weeks, but I'll really miss Christmas Eve Mass."

"Let's have a celebration on the deck of the ship tonight," Agnes proposed.

"Good idea!" Betika agreed.

The two girls constructed a cardboard crib. That night they went up to the deck and under starry skies sang Christmas carols. The three Franciscan sisters came by and stood listening.

"Would you like to join us?" invited Agnes. The sisters smiled and nodded. Together the five of them sang the "Gloria," the song the angels sang when Jesus was born. Then they prayed the rosary. They ended their prayer service with "O Come, All Ye Faithful" sung in Latin. For Agnes there was no better Christmas present than to be headed toward India.

Two days later the ship arrived in Columbo, India. As it neared the shore, Agnes exclaimed, "Oh, it's beautiful, like paradise! Look at those palm trees!"

"And almost every house has plants," Betika added.

"Such poverty, though," Agnes murmured. "Look at those half-naked men pulling carts like horses. I'll never ride in a cart like that!"

"Me neither," promised Betika.

The brother of a Loreto sister met the two girls. He took them to a mission school and then to his house. To their dismay, they rode in a rickshaw, one of the man-drawn carts!

The next evening Agnes and Betika boarded the ship for Darjeeling. This time a priest was a passenger, so daily Mass was celebrated. The ship stopped at Madras. Agnes was shocked to see the extreme poverty there. Families were living on the streets on palm-leaf mats or on the bare ground. Many people were naked or wore only a ragged loincloth.

On January 6 the ship began its trip up the Ganges River through Agnes's new country, Bengal. That day Agnes wrote her first letter to the *Catholic Mission*, telling of her experiences in India.

When the postulants arrived at their final port, Indian sisters were there to welcome them. Agnes's heart was bursting with joy as she stepped onto the soil of Bengal for the first time.

A week later, the two girls were on a crowded train bound for Darjeeling, "the city of lightning," a resort in the Himalaya Mountains. There, in the shadow of the snow-covered Mount Kanchenjunga, Agnes would make her two-year novitiate.

After a few months of preparation, Agnes was accepted into the novitiate on May 23, 1929. On that day she officially became Sister Teresa of the Child Jesus. Betika became Sister Mary Magdalen. When people asked Agnes, "Who is your patron saint?" she would reply, "Not the big St. Teresa but the little one." The "big one" was St. Teresa of Avila. The "little one" was St. Therese of Lisieux, known as the Little Flower. (St. Therese was a Carmelite nun who taught "a little way" of doing small things well for God. After her death at age twenty-four, she was declared a patron saint of missionaries.) To avoid confusion, Loreto sisters were not to have the same name. Because the community already had a Sister Therese, Agnes spelled her name Teresa.

The archbishop of Calcutta was present at the ceremony in which the postulants became novices. Sister Teresa sent her aunt a photo of herself. On the back she wrote, "My dear aunt, I am fit and well. I send you this photo as a memento of the greatest day of my life: that on which I became wholly Christ's. Much love from your Agnes, little Teresa of the Child Jesus."

Under the guidance of their novice director, the young sisters learned about prayer. Once a week they went to confession. The novices also taught poor children for two hours every day. Sister Teresa began teaching in a school for upper class children in Darjeeling. For a short time she also helped in a small medical station. She wrote for the *Catholic Mission*: "The tiny veranda is always full of the sick, the wretched, and the miserable. All eyes are fixed, full of hope, on me. . . . Many have come from a distance, walking for as much as three hours."

The novices also learned about the history and spirit of their order. Their teacher explained, "The Loreto Sisters is a very old religious congregation. We were founded by Mary Ward in 1609. Mary, who originally lived in England, wanted to consecrate herself to God as a sister and serve the poor."

At this, Teresa's eyes lit up. For sure she was in the right community. Its purpose matched her dream.

Sister continued, "When Catholic persecution in England prevented Mary from taking up religious life, she moved to Flanders. There she began her community. Mary was a mover and a shaker. In those days sisters were usually enclosed and seldom left the convent. Mary received special permission not to be enclosed so that she could minister to the poor. Her community opened a school in London in 1639.

"We sisters in Ireland are a branch of Mary's community. In 1841 we opened a house in Calcutta, where we staff schools and offer medical services."

"Why are we called Loreto Sisters?" Sister Mary Magdalen asked.

"That's a good question," Sister replied. "There is a tradition that the house of the Holy Family was miraculously brought from Nazareth to Loreto, Italy, and later called the Holy House of Loreto. We're named for this house."

Besides prayer and history, Sister Teresa and her companions were trying to master English. They also began to learn Bengali, an Indian language, as well as a little Hindi. There was not much time to be homesick!

On March 24, 1931, Teresa made her first, or temporary, vows of poverty, chastity, and obedience. It would be six years before she made final vows. In the meantime, Sister Teresa was sent to Calcutta to attend college and get a teaching certificate.

She could never have imagined what she would find there….

6

CALCUTTA

When Sister Teresa arrived in India, it was still a colony of England. Calcutta was a large city, second only to London in British lands. In India there were definite class distinctions. These divisions of society were known as castes. Calcutta was crowded with many lower caste people and refugees.

The Loreto Sisters had used money that a Protestant planter left them to purchase property in Entally, a poor eastern suburb of Calcutta. On this property the sisters established two boarding schools for high school girls. One was Loreto Entally for English girls, especially those with problems; the other was St. Mary's for Bengali students from middle-class families. Beyond the school wall lay the slums.

Sister Teresa was sent to teach geography and history at St. Mary's. She taught well and with enthusiasm, and then did her share of supervising the boarders after hours.

One day two sisters were walking in the yard.

"I don't know how Sister Teresa does all she does and stays so happy," one commented.

"Yes, she's not only preparing for her university examinations, but she's helping ten other sisters with their studies. And all this in addition to teaching!" replied the other, shaking her head.

"Did you hear what she's doing now?" asked the first. "She's still teaching at St. Mary's but is going to begin teaching at St. Teresa's too! She'll walk there every day."

"Maybe Albanians are tougher than ordinary people," suggested the other.

"Maybe she's powered with special grace," replied the first. "I've never seen anyone pray with such devotion as Sister Teresa."

St. Teresa School was outside the convent walls. On her way there, Sister Teresa came face to face with the many people who lived in wretched poverty. Making her way around the cows, which roamed freely, Teresa passed people living in squalor on the streets. She saw their makeshift homes on the ground and smelled the odors of filth and disease.

On her first day at St. Teresa's, fifty-two children stared at her. Sister Teresa rolled up her sleeves, found water and a broom, and began sweeping the floor, something that lower caste people do. "What is she," one boy whispered, "a demon or a goddess?" As Sister Teresa cheerfully cleaned, the girls, one by one, volunteered to help, while the boys fetched more water. Two hours later the classroom was ready.

A few years later an Englishman visited the school. Although there were 375 children in two rooms, silence reigned. "What punishment do you use to keep the children in such good order?" the visitor asked Sister Teresa.

Teresa replied, "Their greatest punishment is to have me ignore them. If I allow them to do what they like without my taking any interest, they know they have saddened me. There is no need to use physical punishment. They get plenty of that at home."

Smiling, the Englishman commented, "The children must love you very much, for you love them and at the same time you are working for their good."

On Sundays Sister Teresa visited the slums, where some families lived in a single room. The children stared at her in silence until she gently stroked each dirty little head. She won their hearts. They began to call her "Ma."

Teresa made her final vows, vows for life, in May of 1937. After a Loreto Sister made her final vows, she was called by the title "Mother" instead of "Sister." Hearing that Sister Teresa was leaving to become "Mother" Teresa, a young boy came to her in tears. "Oh, don't become Mother!" he wailed. Sister Teresa hugged him and said, "What's the matter? Don't worry. I will be back. I will always be your Ma." The little boy smiled in relief and went skipping back to his friends.

On the day that Sister Teresa and Sister Mary Magdalen made their final vows, a Jesuit seminarian wrote to his provincial superior, Father Jambrenkovic. He reported, "Obviously they are both very happy, and you helped them to achieve this happiness, since it was thanks to you that Sister Teresa was able to come to India."

Right after vows, Mother Teresa was appointed superior of St. Mary's School. A year later she was made principal. When her mother heard the news, she wrote, "Dear child, do not forget that you went out to India for the sake of the poor." Mrs. Bojaxhiu's words echoed what Teresa was already feeling. As she walked the streets of Bengal, she wondered why she was teaching children of well-to-do families while there were so many others in greater need. Gradually an idea began to take shape in her mind and heart: God meant her to serve the poorest of the poor.

7

THE SECOND CALL

It was September 10, 1946. Mother Teresa had taught in Entally for fifteen years. In addition she was head of the Daughters of St. Anne, a diocesan community of Bengali sisters who taught at St. Mary's. These sisters wore blue saris and worked directly with the poor. Mother Teresa also helped Father Henry, pastor of St. Teresa Church, with a sodality. The girls in the sodality visited hospitals and the Motijhil slums.

Now Teresa was on a train traveling four hundred miles to Darjeeling to make her annual retreat. (It's Church law that vowed men and women spend a week each year in silence and prayer.)

Rocked back and forth by the movement of the train and lulled by the clickety-clack of the wheels on the track, Mother Teresa let her mind wander. Perhaps she thought of her family. In 1932 Aga had moved to Tirana, Albania where Lazar was living. She had become a translator and then a radio announcer. Two years later their mother had joined them. The family knew that their Gonxha was always praying for them. In 1939, when Albania was invaded by Italy, Lazar moved to Italy. He had married and now had a family of his own.

Suddenly, Teresa's thoughts were interrupted. Surrounded by people on the crowded train, she clearly heard God's voice speak within her: "You must leave the convent to help the poor by living among them." Mother Teresa was astonished. God was calling her to something new. It was a call within her call to be a sister.

All during her retreat Teresa prayed over and pondered God's message. It became clearer and clearer that God wanted her to be poor and to love him in the distressing disguise of the poorest of the poor.

Back in Entally she told the other sisters what had happened. "I know where I belong, but I don't know how to get there," Teresa explained.

One day Archbishop Perier visited the convent.

"Archbishop," one sister said, "there's a young sister here who has an unusual desire."

"You must leave the convent to help the poor…"

"Yes," another chimed in, "Mother Teresa believes that God is sending her on a special mission. Would you speak with her?"

"Have her make an appointment to see me," the archbishop graciously replied.

The archbishop met with Mother Teresa and listened to her story. At the end he leaned forward in his chair. "I can't let you do this yet, Mother," he quietly concluded.

When Teresa returned from the meeting, her friends asked, "Well, what happened?"

"The archbishop listened to me but won't do anything yet."

Knowing how Teresa's heart was set on her dream, the sisters offered sympathy.

"But I didn't expect any other reply," Mother Teresa admitted. "An archbishop can't allow a nun to found a new order all of a sudden, as if she's had some sort of unique message from God."

Later when a priest speaking to Archbishop Perier mentioned Teresa's request, the archbishop responded, "How can I let a lone European nun wander the streets when there's so much political turmoil?"

And he was right. At that time India was becoming independent from Britain. The country of Pakistan was carved out of India as a homeland for Muslims. There were bloody riots between Hindus and Muslims. Refugees poured into Calcutta, and food was scarce.

Shortly after Mother Teresa's meeting with the archbishop, she was transferred to another town for reasons of health. When the archbishop learned of this, he said, "Please send Mother Teresa back to Calcutta because we're still discussing her future." He was consulting priests about Teresa's proposal, and they were supportive of her. Father Henry, who worked with Mother Teresa, was especially excited about the idea, even though he had no idea that she was the sister behind it.

Teresa returned to Entally. She arrived just in time to help with a crisis at the school. With her leadership skills, she settled the disagreement between the teachers and the students.

Finally the archbishop asked to see Mother Teresa. "I would like to support you, Mother," he began, "but you know that Rome won't grant permission for a new order if a similar one already exists. Did you ever consider transferring to the Daughters of St. Anne? They work with the poor."

"These sisters do wonderful work," Mother Teresa agreed. "But afterwards they return to their lovely convent. I would like to actually *live* with the poor and share their life."

The archbishop folded his hands on his desk. "I understand," he said. "I will petition Rome to grant your request. But first you must ask your Loreto superior for permission. Write a letter proposing that you leave the community to begin a new order. Don't ask for exclaustration, which would allow you to live outside the convent but still belong to the order."

This directive was hard to take because Teresa wanted to remain a sister. But she did as she was told. Soon the major superior of the Loreto sisters wrote back from Ireland, "If this is the will of God, then I give you permission with all my heart. You can count on the friendship and esteem of all of us here. And if for any reason you want to come back to Loreto, we shall accept you again gladly as our sister."

When Mother Teresa applied to Rome, she was granted exclaustration by Pope Pius XII—even though she hadn't asked for it! She could continue to live under vows, and her superior would be the archbishop of Calcutta.

Teresa was ready to step out alone into her unknown future. Years later she would tell people, "Leaving the Loreto community was the most difficult thing I have ever done. It was a greater sacrifice than leaving my family and my country to enter religious life." She liked to say, "Loreto is everything to me."

8

TOWARD THE DREAM

On August 16, 1948, Father Henry blessed the three white saris which were to be Mother Teresa's habit, or religious dress. They were trimmed in blue with a small black crucifix pinned to the left shoulder. As the priest sprinkled holy water on the saris, some of the sisters were sobbing. Earlier Teresa's students had sung their farewells in a special presentation.

That evening Teresa exchanged her Loreto habit for one of the saris and a pair of sandals. She prayed, entrusting her work to the Immaculate Heart of Mary. Then she walked out the door of the convent and onto the street. In her bag were only five rupees—equivalent to about $1.00 in American money at that time. The archbishop and the Loreto Sisters would give her financial support in the future.

Mother Teresa first went to the city of Patna, 230 miles away, for medical training at the Medical Missionary Sisters' hospital.

In barely three months she learned much. She also met a new friend, Mother Dengal, who was a surgeon. One day Teresa was talking to Mother Dengal about the community she hoped to found. "My sisters and I will eat only rice and salt," she declared. She wanted to live poorly.

Mother Dengal raised her eyebrows. "That would be a mortal sin," the nun warned. "Do you want to help the poor and the sick, or do you want to die with them? Do you want your young nuns to lose their lives, or do you want them healthy and strong, so they can work for Christ?" It was a very good point, and Mother Teresa changed her mind.

In December Teresa returned to Calcutta equipped with nursing skills. She would need them because more poor refugees were settling wherever there was room. The streets were filled with disease, dirt, and death.

At first Mother Teresa stayed at a home for the poor elderly run by the Little Sisters of the Poor. These sisters maintained their houses for the poor by begging. That is exactly how Teresa intended to support her work.

Teresa visited the poor, caring for their sick, cleaning their houses, and washing their clothes. At the same time she looked for a shelter for her work. A week after she arrived back in Calcutta, she found one. In Motijhil, the slum near her old Entally convent, she bought a two-room hut with a door that wouldn't shut. She purchased it with money a parish priest had given her the previous day.

The very day that Teresa obtained the house, she gathered children and began to teach them outside. They had no desks or books. Mother Teresa wrote letters on the ground with a stick. As days passed, three teachers joined her. People donated money, books, and furniture. More and more naked and hungry students learned the alphabet and hygiene. They received milk every day and—as a reward if they were good—a bar of soap. Mother named the school Nirmal Hriday, which means "Place of the Pure Heart" (in honor of the Immaculate Heart of Mary).

After school Mother Teresa visited and cared for the sick, especially those suffering from leprosy. Lepers had ugly sores and were missing fingers and toes. People considered them cursed by God. Once Mother said, "I wouldn't touch a leper for a thousand pounds (British money). Yet I do it willingly for the love of God."

Prayer and determination gave Teresa the strength to labor long hours. She wrote in her diary, "The poverty of the poor is so hard. When I was going and going till my legs and arms were paining, I was thinking how they have to suffer to get food and shelter. Then the comfort of Loreto came to tempt me, but of my own free choice, my God, and out of love for you, I desire to remain and do whatever is your holy will in my regard. Give me courage now, this moment."

One day a child said to Mother Teresa, "You know, Sister, Zena and her brother have had nothing to eat since yesterday morning and will have nothing tonight." Teresa brought rice and two eggs and made a meal for the children.

That evening she stopped at a church and asked the priest for a donation. The priest criticized her. "I don't understand how you can do what you're doing," he said. "You should be receiving financial backing from a parish priest." He left without even saying goodbye. Walking home, Teresa cried at the humiliating refusal.

A teacher from St. Mary's came to help at Mother Teresa's school. So did some girls whom Teresa had taught. A few weeks after beginning her school, Mother Teresa set up a dispensary where people could come to receive free medicine. Located in a class-room of St. Teresa's school, the dispensary opened after school hours. A few days later, Mother Teresa decided to open a second school, one in Tiljala. Soon six children there were kept out of mischief by attending classes. People began to call Teresa "the Slum Sister."

As the number of students grew, so did the number of helpers. One day Teresa re-marked to her spiritual director, Father van Exem, "We really need another place to live, one that's not so far from our work."

"I agree," Father said. "It takes an hour to walk from Motijhil to your place." He knew that Mother Teresa would always give her bus money away to a poor person and walk home.

God was just about to answer Teresa's prayers.

9

CREEK STREET HOME

Father van Exem was visiting an Indian parishioner, Michael Gomes, in his three-storied home at 14 Creek Street. Mr. Gomes's eight-year-old daughter, Mabel, sat quietly listening to the two men.

"Michael," Father van Exem said, "can you think of some place where Mother Teresa and her work can be housed? Maybe a mud hut, a shanty, something simple that's nearby?"

Mabel piped up, "Father, the whole upstairs is empty. It's not being used. Mother Teresa could come here and stay with us!"

"That's an idea. Let's take a look," Mr. Gomes said to Father van Exem. The two went upstairs and surveyed the rooms.

"I'm afraid this is too grand for Mother Teresa," Father concluded. "But how much would you charge her for rent?"

"Nothing," Mr. Gomes assured him.

"Still, I don't think she would accept it," said Father van Exem.

When Teresa heard about the offer, however, she gladly and gratefully accepted it. She moved in along with a widow, the cook at St. Mary's, who helped her. Right after they settled in, Mother Teresa was ready to visit the poor and suffering. "Would you like to come with me?" she invited Mabel.

"Oh, yes!" the little girl replied.

Mr. Gomes also became involved in Teresa's work. He went with her to beg medicines. One day the two entered a pharmacy with a long list of needed medicines. The pharmacist was surrounded by people clamoring for attention. When it was Mother Teresa's turn, she showed him the list and asked, "Would you please give us these medicines for free, for the poor?"

The pharmacist replied, "Madam, you have come to the wrong door. Let me get on with my work."

Mother Teresa and Mr. Gomes went outside and sat down. Teresa began praying the rosary. Suddenly the pharmacist appeared carrying three packages.

"Here is the medicine that you need," he said. "Consider it a gift."

Another day Mother Teresa herself became ill and had a high fever. Delirious, she imagined that she had died and gone before St. Peter, the keeper of the gates of heaven. "Return home," St. Peter told her. "There are no slums in heaven."

"Then I'll fill heaven with my people from the slums!" Teresa responded.

10

FIRST MISSIONARIES OF CHARITY

One day a former student from St. Mary's came to visit Mother Teresa. Her name was Subhasini Das, and she was a Bengali girl from a well-to-do family. The two were delighted to see each other.

After the happy greetings were over, Subhasini blurted out, "Mother, I've come to live with you."

Mother Teresa glanced at the girl's silk sari and smiled. She held out her rough hands, then gestured toward her wrinkled, plain habit. She pointed to the house and its poor residents. "Very well, my daughter," Mother said, "you see my hands and my clothes. Compare them with yours. Religious life, especially this kind, demands a high degree of sacrifice. A nun must forget herself completely in order to dedicate herself to God and her neighbor."

"I understand," Subhasini replied eagerly. "I have thought about it for a long time. I'm ready. I beg you to accept me."

"Come back later after you've considered things more," Mother gently advised.

With that Subhasini left.

On March 19, 1949, there was a knock on the door. When Mother Teresa opened it, there stood Subhasini dressed in simple clothes and wearing no jewelry.

"Here I am, Mother," she said. "I have come as you told me to. I beg you not to refuse me this time. I have made a decision deep down in my heart."

Subhasini became the first to join Mother Teresa in what was to become the Congregation of the Missionaries of Charity. As a sister, Subhasini adopted Mother Teresa's baptismal name and became Sister Agnes.

Two months later there were three sisters with Mother Teresa. By that November there were five. In 1950 there were seven. The Sisters of Loreto helped Mother with financial support. Some of them even transferred into her new community.

For a new congregation to be officially recognized by the Church, it must have at least ten members and an approved rule or constitution. A constitution contains a community's principles of operation and spiritual goals. With the help of priest friends, Mother Teresa wrote her congregation's constitution. These are its opening sentences:

"Our objective is to quench the thirst of Jesus Christ on the cross by dedicating ourselves freely to serve the poorest of the poor, according to the work and teaching of Our Lord, thus announcing the Kingdom of God in a special way.

"Our special mission is to work for the salvation and holiness of the poorest of the poor. As Jesus was sent by the Father, so he sends us, full of his spirit, to proclaim the gospel of his love and pity among the poorest of the poor throughout the world."

The Missionaries of Charity would also make a fourth vow. In addition to poverty, chastity, and obedience, they would vow wholehearted and free service to the poorest of the poor. Above the crucifix in the chapels of each of their houses they would place the words of Jesus: "I thirst."

The sisters would not accept government support for themselves. Neither would they accept any financial assistance from the Church. Mother Teresa explained, "I do not want any material security for our sisters. We do not want to have any bank accounts, or any assured means of subsistence. We must proceed with hope in Divine Providence." Teresa believed that the Lord who cared for the flowers and grass would take much greater care of her sisters.

Mother Teresa dedicated her new community to the Immaculate Heart of Mary. The archbishop of Calcutta sent the constitution to Rome, and Pope Pius XII approved it in the fall of 1950. The Congregation of the Missionaries of Charity would have its motherhouse at 14 Creek Street, Calcutta. Today the congregation celebrates the anniversary of its founding on October 7, the Feast of Our Lady of the Rosary, because on this day the formal declaration of the founding was read at a Mass celebrated by the archbishop. There were twelve sisters in the original group. Mother Teresa now added the community initials after her name. She became Mother Teresa, M.C.

With these first sisters, Mother shared her dream for the community. She told them, "We shall weave a chain of love around the world—yes, a chain of love." On a sheet of paper she drew the world and encircled it with rosary beads. The cross fell on Calcutta. This design became the community logo.

Just as Mother Teresa had warned Sister Agnes, the community led a strict life. The

"We shall weave a chain of love around the world."

sisters rose at 4:40 A.M. At 5:00 A.M. they began their prayers in chapel. This was followed by the celebration of the Eucharist. After breakfast and housecleaning, the sisters served the poor from 8:00 to 12:30. After lunch, they took a brief rest. Then came a period of spiritual reading and meditation, followed by tea. From 3:15 to 4:30 there was adoration of the Blessed Sacrament. The sisters then went out again to serve the poor until 7:30. After supper there were evening prayers at 9:00 P.M. The sisters retired at 9:45.

Although temperatures in Calcutta often rose above 100 degrees, Mother Teresa and her sisters had no fans or refrigerators. They each owned only two saris and a pail to wash them in, a plate and basic utensils. They slept in a dormitory instead of in individual bedrooms. Mother Teresa wanted them to live like the poor people they served.

Despite the hardships, the sisters were happy. Michael Gomes often heard the young sisters laughing and playing games in their upstairs apartment.

11

THE NEW MOTHERHOUSE

The new community soon outgrew the house on Creek Street, but there was no money to buy a larger house. So the sisters did what they could—they prayed. Mother Teresa even made a novena to St. Cecilia.

Soon Father Henry heard that a Muslim was moving to Pakistan and selling his house. It was a beautiful building in the center of the city.

Father paid a visit to the man. "How much are you asking for your property?" he asked.

"Make me an offer," the man replied.

Father quoted the largest figure he could (the sum that Archbishop Perier had promised to lend Mother Teresa), but it was an amount that would not even cover the land on which the house stood.

The Muslim gentleman went to pray. When he returned, he said, "I accept your offer. God gave me this house. I will give it back to him."

Three days later Father Henry took Mother Teresa to see the house, which consisted of three combined buildings. When she saw it, she exclaimed, "Father, it's too big! What will we do with all that?"

The priest responded, "Mother, you *will* need it all. There will come a day when you will ask where you can put all your people."

And so the house at 54a Lower Circular Road, Calcutta, became the motherhouse of the Missionaries of Charity. In a few years the chapel would be filled every morning and evening with sisters in white saris sitting close to each other on the floor, facing the tabernacle and altar. Thousands of girls would someday make their vows there as Missionaries of Charity, wearing a garland of flowers that day as Indian brides do. Every one of them would be steeped in the love of Jesus in the tradition of their Mother, who wrote this prayer:

He is the Life that I want to live.
He is the Light that I want to radiate.
He is the Way to the Father.
He is the Love with which I want to love.
He is the Joy that I want to share.
He is the Peace that I want to sow.
Jesus is Everything to me.
Without Him, I can do nothing.

12

PLACE OF THE PURE HEART

One day Michael Gomes and Mother Teresa were traveling during a heavy downpour. They came upon a man dying on the roadside. Since Campbell Hospital was right there, they entered it and asked the authorities to take the man in. "Sorry," they were told. "We can't admit him." Mr. Gomes and Mother went to purchase medicine for the man. By the time they returned with it, he was dead.

Frustrated and angry, Mother Teresa exclaimed, "They look after a dog or a cat better than a fellow human being! They would not allow this to happen to their pets." Hospitals in India were crowded and preferred to take in people likely to recover rather than the dying.

Mother Teresa was determined to take care of those dying on the streets. She went to the police commissioner and complained about the situation. She went to the health commissioner and begged, "Give me at least a room."

Realizing that this woman could relieve an embarrassing situation for the city, the Calcutta officials acted. In 1952 Mother Teresa was given a wing in a rest house for pilgrims attached to the temple of the Goddess Kali in the town of Kalighat. Mother gave the home the same name as her first school: Nirmal Hriday—Place of the Pure Heart (in honor of the Immaculate Heart of Mary.) The hospital had two wards. One could hold sixty men, the other sixty women. Low pallets were arranged close together in long rows with numbers painted on the wall behind them. The beds were soon filled with people who were only skin and bones. The patients were brought in by the police or carried in by the sisters and their helpers.

In Nirmal Hriday the sisters and their volunteers treated the dying with gentleness and love. Dying persons were washed, fed, consoled, encouraged, and prepared for death. One man covered with sores commented, "I've lived like an animal in the street, but I will die like an angel." Mother Teresa had brought him in from an open drain on the street. Three hours later he died

All patients of the Missionaries of Charity die and are buried according to the customs of their own religion. Mother Teresa did not intend to make everyone a Catholic convert. She said, "If in coming face to face with God we accept him in our lives, then we are converting. We become a better Hindu, a better Muslim, a better Catholic, a better whatever we are."

Even though this was Mother's position, some young people went to a civic leader and complained, "That foreign woman is converting the dying to Christianity. How can you allow this?"

"I'll see her and get her out," the leader promised.

The man visited Nirmal Hriday and observed how the dying were treated. He went to Mother Teresa, took her hand, and said, "Keep on with your work. I wish you good luck and success. May God help you!"

After he left, he told the accusers, "I promised I would get that woman out of there, and I shall. But I shall not get her out of that place before you get your mothers and sisters to do the work these nuns are doing. In the temple you have a goddess in stone. Here you have a living goddess!"

A journalist named Malcolm Muggeridge came one day to do a documentary film on Nirmal Hriday. He and his crew observed the workers giving injections, scrubbing floors, changing bedclothes, feeding people, shaving the gaunt men, and holding the dying. The rooms were dim because the windows were high up in the walls. When it was time to shoot the pictures, Ken, the photographer, commented, "There's not enough light in here. I only have one small light with me. The pictures won't take."

"Try it anyway," Malcolm directed, even though he knew Ken was right.

"It's impossible to shoot here," Ken insisted. "I'll do it, but I'll also film scenes outside in the sunlight."

When the film was developed, the scenes inside Nirmal Hriday were bathed in a beautiful, soft glow! On the other hand, the outside scenes were dim. Ken couldn't explain it. Malcolm said, "I believe that the light is the love that fills the hospital." In a book he wrote on Mother Teresa, Malcolm Muggeridge stated, "I am personally persuaded that Ken recorded the first authentic photographic miracle."

13

A HOME FOR CHILDREN

For some time Mother Teresa wished to open a home to care for unwanted children. One day she spoke to Father Edward Le Joly. He was a Jesuit missionary from Belgium who was the spiritual director of her novices. She said, "Mrs. X asked me to pray that her husband may stop drinking. He drinks a bottle of whisky—which costs ninety rupees—every day. If he can pay ninety rupees per day for his drinks, I can pay five hundred rupees a month for that house on Lower Circular Road that is up for rent! I'll take it and start a children's home."

In 1955 Mother Teresa began Shishu Bhavan for abandoned infants. These unwanted babies were left on the doorstep, brought by the police or other people, or found in the rubbish dumps. Some infants suffered mental or physical handicaps. They were born premature or harmed by attempted abortions or their mother's drug use.

In Shishu Bhavan the babies received loving care. Some of them died within an hour after they were brought in. Mother Teresa explained, "Even an infant can feel human warmth. This is why a dying child must be loved and comforted." Other children became healthy and were adopted. Some children grew up in the home. The sisters paid for their education and helped them to get a job and marry. Girls were even provided a dowry. The sisters liked to say, "Anyone who marries one of our children has twenty mothers-in-law!"

The home had two other purposes. It served as a shelter for unwed mothers awaiting their babies. While they waited, the young women helped with the work. At Shishu Bhavan food was also distributed to the poor. It was the only meal that some women and children had.

Shishu Bhavans multiplied. They are bright, happy places built near the convents so the sisters can provide constant care for premature and sick children. Mother Teresa established children's homes in the leprosy centers too.

The homes house from twenty to two hundred children. Mother Teresa often said, "If there is an unwanted baby, don't let it die. Send it to me." To a visitor at a home Mother might say, "There's a joke in Calcutta: Mother Teresa talks about family planning, but she certainly doesn't practice it. Every day she has more and more children!" Then Mother Teresa would put her hands on her waist and double up with laughter.

Later Mother Teresa was outspoken when it came to defending the unborn. On February 3, 1994, she gave an address at the National Prayer Breakfast in Washington, D.C. President Clinton and his wife Hillary were present. Mother spoke at length and bluntly about abortion. She said, "Any country that accepts abortion is teaching its people not to love, but to use violence to get what they want." Her words made some of the dignitaries at the breakfast very uncomfortable.

Previously Mother Teresa had written to the United States Supreme Court, arguing against abortion. Her stance is summed up in her often-quoted statement, "It is a poverty to decide that a child must die so that you may live as you wish."

14

CITY OF PEACE

Many Christians and non-Christians were attracted to Mother Teresa's works and came to help. The sisters didn't own any cars of their own. They frequented the public transportation used by the poor. An American priest used offerings he received to celebrate Masses to purchase for Mother Teresa and her sisters their first ambulance.

Mother Teresa focused on lepers in particular. Millions of people in India suffer from leprosy. This is a dreaded and contagious disease that eats away parts of the body and causes a terrible odor. Many people in India thought that leprosy was the result of sin. Lepers were outcasts of society. Often their families would have nothing to do with them.

Perhaps Mother was thinking of lepers when she instructed her sisters, "Let each sister see Jesus Christ in the person of the poor. The more repugnant the work or the person, the greater also must be her faith, love, and cheerful devotion in ministering to our Lord in this distressing disguise."

The first thing that Mother Teresa did for lepers was to obtain a mobile clinic. "It's hard for the lepers to get to us," she explained. "We must go to them." From this clinic she and her sisters washed the wounds and changed the bandages of thousands of lepers.

Mother's concern for lepers was heightened when a leper ghetto was being moved for the sake of city planning. The lepers were slated to be moved to a region that had little water. Mother Teresa spoke out on their behalf. The lepers still had to move, but not until the area was made more inhabitable.

A result of this crisis was Mother Teresa's declaring Leper Collection Day in 1957. She sent offering collection jars throughout the city with the slogan, "Touch a leper with your kindness." People were generous. The money collected helped her start Shanti Nager—City of Peace—on thirty-four acres of land the government gave her for this purpose. In this city lepers could live, receive treatment, and be prepared to reenter society. Sister Francis Xavier, a Yugoslav doctor, took charge of the project.

*"The greatest disease is to be unwanted
and unloved."*

At the centers for lepers run by the Missionaries of Charity, people—even those who have only stumps instead of hands and feet—are helped to earn a living.

Visiting the lepers one day, Mother Teresa told them, "God loves you very specially. God is close to you. Your illness is no sin." One old man walked up to Mother Teresa with great difficulty and said, "Please, say that again. I never heard anything like it before. I've only heard that nobody wanted me. How beautiful it is to know that God loves me!"

Mother Teresa often repeated, "The greatest disease is to be unwanted, unloved, just left alone, a throwaway of society."

The Archbishop of Calcutta, Henry D'Souza, once summed up Mother Teresa's life in these words: "Perhaps the greatest message she has given is the value and dignity of human life. All human life is precious."

15

GROWTH

At first Mother Teresa formed her novices herself. She taught them about religious life and passed on to them her spirituality and values. For instance, she might say to them, "No one should leave you without feeling better and happier. For the sick each of us must be a ray of God's goodness. We must always be ready to smile at the children whom we gather up and help. We must be ever ready to smile at all the rejected people we love and serve and keep company with. We should give far too little if we handed out medicine only and not our heart." Another time she might encourage the novices, "Give until it hurts—with a smile!"

Later Sister Agnes became the novice director. Mother Teresa asked Father Edward Le Joly to be a spiritual father for the novices and to hear their confessions. When he first came, there were thirty-five novices. The next year there were fifty. The community continued to grow by leaps and bounds. So did its places of ministry.

A journalist once asked, "Mother Teresa, what would you consider to be most important in the formation of nuns today?"

Without hesitation Mother replied, "What is most important is to train the sisters to a deep, personal love for the Blessed Sacrament, so that they may find Jesus in the Eucharist. Then they will go out and find Jesus in their neighbor, and they will serve him in the poor."

Jesus gave us himself as food and drink. Mother Teresa would exhort her sisters to do the same. "Let the people eat you up," she would say.

Mother Teresa yearned to open houses of her congregation beyond the diocese of Calcutta. Church law, however, required a ten-year wait before a new congregation expanded. In 1960 when Mother Teresa was free to open a new house, she did so in Ranchi. Then she started a house in Delhi. Prime Minister Nehru came to its opening although he had been ill and in bed. Mother Teresa asked the distinguished guest, "Can I tell you about our work?"

Nehru shook his head and said, "No, Mother, you needn't tell me about your work. I know about it. That is why I have come."

That same year was memorable for another reason. Mother Teresa traveled to Italy and visited her brother Lazar, whom she hadn't seen since 1924. She met his wife and their daughter Aga and her husband. Mother Teresa and Lazar enjoyed recalling memories and catching up on their lives. They even faced a problem together.

"Look at these letters from Mother and Aga," Lazar said, handing his sister sheets of stationery. "They want to see us very badly, but they are trapped there in Albania. Aga gets lonely and depressed."

"The situation in Albania is getting worse and worse," replied Mother Teresa, her large, brown eyes full of sadness. "The country has cut itself off from the rest of the world. It's almost impossible to cross its borders to enter or leave."

"It's becoming an atheistic state," Lazar added. "Religion is being suppressed. Don't give up hope, though. Our friends may be able to work something out so that we can visit Mother and Aga or get them out of the country."

Although Albania didn't welcome Mother Teresa, many other countries did.

The first house established outside of India was the idea of the Pope's representative to New Delhi. He had learned that in Venezuela people of African descent had no land and needed help. He asked Archbishop Perier if the sisters could go. The archbishop could hardly refuse. That same year, 1965, Mother Teresa's congregation became a pontifical institute. That meant that the sisters were no longer under the authority of the archbishop of Calcutta, but directly under the Pope.

In 1968 Pope Paul VI wrote Mother Teresa and invited her to open a house in Rome. Enclosed with the letter were a round-trip ticket to Rome and $10,000. Mother visited Rome, saw the great needs, and opened the first of several houses there. After this, two houses were opened in Australia, one for alcoholics and drug addicts and one for aborigines, the native people of Australia. Since 1970 the Missionaries of Charity have opened houses in many countries at the invitation of local bishops. In Ethiopia, however, it took an interview with Emperor Haile Selassie before Mother Teresa was allowed to open a mission there.

Throughout these years of marvelous growth, Mother Teresa had one heartache. She was not able to grant her mother's wish and visit her.

16

BRANCHING OUT

Mother Teresa's work for the poorest of the poor spread even beyond the congregation of sisters she had founded. One morning back in 1954, Ann Blaikie, the wife of a British businessman, had come to the convent and asked to see Mother Teresa.

"Mother," Ann said, when the tiny nun entered the room. "I'm so glad to meet you. I read about your work and I'd like to help."

"How wonderful!" exclaimed Mother Teresa. "Thank God. Let's visit our Home for the Dying."

Without further ado, Mother and Ann climbed into an old van and were on their way. This was the first stage of Ann's journey of founding the Co-Workers of Mother Teresa. She eventually gathered other people who helped collect toys and clothes for needy children for Christmas. Afterwards, Mother Teresa visited this first group of Co-Workers. "Thank you for giving our children a merry Christmas," she said, "God will bless you. Now the Hindu and Muslim feasts are coming soon. These children could use gifts too."

"We'll collect them," Ann and the others responded.

The society grew. When Ann returned to England, she began a Co-Worker group there. Soon groups formed wherever Mother Teresa's houses were. In 1969 the International Association of Co-Workers of Mother Teresa was officially established and blessed by Pope Paul VI. The members are now organized under a constitution and meet once a month. They not only help with the sisters' work, but they pray, do small acts of kindness for others, and promise to live simply without luxury. Some Co-Worker groups are Hindu.

When Mother Teresa was receiving medical training in Patna after she first left the Loreto convent, she had met Jacqueline de Decker. Jacqueline was a young Belgian woman who shared Mother's dream of living with and serving the poor. "She is my second self," Mother Teresa liked to say. Jacqueline, however, became very ill and had to return to Europe. There she realized that God was calling her to offer her life of suffering and pain for Mother Teresa's work. Mother wrote to her in 1952, "The work here is tremendous and needs workers, it is true, but I need souls like yours to pray and suffer for it."

Jacqueline went on to find sick persons willing to be spiritually linked to a Missionary of Charity. She paired each sister with a suffering person who would pray for her, write her, and offer his or her suffering for the success of her work with the poor. This was the beginning of the Sick and Suffering Co-Workers, who have now spread all over the world.

A masculine branch of the Missionaries of Charity, called the Missionary Brothers of Charity, developed out of necessity. In 1961 Mother Teresa had explained to Father van Exem, "The boys in Shishu Bhawan are growing up. We sisters will have difficulty looking after them. Also, in our work with the lepers, there are some tasks that are better suited to men. What do you think about starting a congregation of brothers?"

"I think it's an excellent idea," Father van Exem replied. Looking down on Mother Teresa, who was barely five feet tall, he wondered how she even managed to handle the physical demands of her work.

In no time at all the archbishop approved the plan, and six young men began helping at Shishu Bhawan. The new community of brothers was established in 1963. Because the Church does not allow a woman to be head of a men's congregation, Mother Teresa searched for a leader. A tall, thin, thirty-eight-year-old Jesuit priest from Australia had a strong desire to work for the poor. He asked to become a Missionary Brother of Charity right before making final vows. The Jesuits released him from their order, and in 1965 he became Brother Andrew.

The brothers moved to their own house, which Mother Teresa purchased. They lived essentially according to her rule. She instructed them, "What you do, Brothers, as religious is from Jesus, by Jesus, for Jesus." The brothers, though, were freer than the sisters to go about doing their work. The first work they undertook was to minister to the hundreds of boys and young men who lived at the railway station. The brothers began houses where the boys were trained for jobs. They also worked at the large leper colony. Soon the brothers spread to other countries too, beginning with Vietnam.

But Mother Teresa's family was not yet complete. Convinced that prayer is essential to sustain her work, she envisioned a center that would be a powerhouse of prayer. The sisters who lived there would devote themselves to prayer. For this purpose, in 1976 in the Bronx, New York she founded the Missionary Sisters of the Word. These sisters ponder the word of God through the Eucharist and meditation. Then they announce it by being present to and helping the needy several hours a day. Mother Teresa founded the male counterpart in Rome: the Missionary Brothers of the Word. The Church did not consider this group a congregation but a pious institute.

In 1977 Mother merged the Sisters of the Word with her first community, saying, "There are no more Sisters of the Word. There are only Missionaries of Charity comprising two wings: one active, one contemplative."

Mother Teresa did what she did with the help of many people. She explained, "I can do what you cannot; you can do what I cannot. Together we can do something beautiful for God."

17

A FAMILY CROSS

Mother Teresa finally visited Yugoslavia in 1972. Imagine her thoughts and feelings as she returned to her country and her beloved city of Skopje for the first time in forty-four years!

In 1963 an earthquake had struck Skopje, destroying many homes as well as Sacred Heart of Jesus Church. Her own family home had been demolished. From Skopje Mother Teresa traveled to Letnice. There she prayed before the statue of the Madonna as she had done so many times as a girl.

That year was a sad one for Mother Teresa. Two years earlier her sister Aga had written to say that their mother had lost a lot of weight. Aga reported that on some days Mrs. Bojaxhiu didn't even recognize her. Then Mrs. Bojaxhiu herself had written to Lazar: "My only wish is to see your family and my dear Agnes before I die."

Mother Teresa did her best to bring her family together. In Rome she went to the Albanian Embassy to ask permission to visit

Albania. Mrs. Eileen Egan, a friend who was the Inspector for Catholic Relief Services in India, accompanied her. Later Mrs. Egan reported, "They would not even speak to her. When Mother Teresa left the embassy, for the first time I saw tears in her eyes. She looked up towards heaven and said, 'O, God, I understand and accept my own sufferings. But it is hard to understand and accept my mother's, when all she desires in her old age is to see her children again.'"

The next day Mrs. Bojaxhiu dictated a letter to Aga. She wrote, "Even if we never meet again in this sad world, we shall surely meet in heaven."

Mother Teresa and powerful leaders of countries tried to sway the Albanian Embassy's decision not to allow her into the country. Nothing helped. She had to tell Lazar, "Up to now I have managed to obtain everything through love and prayer . . . but there are still walls and obstacles that even love cannot knock down."

Back in Calcutta, Mother Teresa received a telegram from Lazar. It read: "Pray for Mother who died on July 12." Mother Teresa took the telegram with her to chapel and remained there a long time.

Aga, now alone in Albania, missed her mother very much. She wrote to Mother Teresa about her plan to leave the country. Her request was denied. She never saw Lazar or Mother Teresa again. Only three years after her mother passed away, Aga also died.

The strong faith and Gospel values that Mother Teresa had learned in her own family continued to guide her in forming her new family of sisters.

18

AROUND THE WORLD

Mother Teresa and her sisters heard the cries of the poor throughout the world. They settled in the slums of Rome and worked to help the gypsies. In Australia the sisters opened a home for the rehabilitation of drug addicts. The Missionaries of Charity began a home for the sick and elderly and addicts and alcoholics in London

In 1962 Mother Teresa founded a home for abandoned children in Bombay. Later a newspaper reported, "Now in Bombay nobody dies all alone in the streets. Mother Teresa, a woman small in stature but great in spirit, battles, with her sisters, against death, leprosy, and poverty. This is a divine gift for us."

The Eucharistic Congress was held in Bombay in 1964. Pope Paul VI was present for it. Mother Teresa was on her way to attend the opening ceremony when she saw a married couple dying in the street. Extremely thin and with bloody faces, they were helping each other move along. Mother Teresa took them by the hand. The man said a few words and died in her arms. Carrying the wife on her shoulders, Mother Teresa brought her to the home for the dying.

Although she missed the Pope that day, he singled her out afterwards. An American had given him a Lincoln limousine for his travels in India. Before the Holy Father left Bombay he said, "I wish to donate this white motorcar to Mother Teresa, the superior general of the Missionaries of Charity, to help her in her great work of love." But Mother Teresa was a shrewd businesswoman. She held a raffle for the car and made five times more money than she would have if she had sold it! The profit was used for the lepers' City of Peace.

In 1968 the sisters opened their first house in Tanzania in Africa. Mother Teresa said, "Africa is a continent materially poor but spiritually rich. Poor, but offering great opportunities for the apostolate."

Mother Teresa wanted to open a novitiate in Europe. In 1970 she looked for a house in London and found one for 6,500 pounds. The sisters begged for money, even over the radio. When they counted the donations they received, they totaled exactly 6,500 pounds! Later this novitiate was moved to Rome.

The sisters worked among the Muslims too. In 1970 they moved into Jordan and in 1973 into Gaza in Israel to help the Palestinians. The sisters were the first Catholics to enter Yemen, a Muslim country where Christian symbols are banned. There they cared mostly for lepers.

Once when Mother Teresa could not afford airline tickets she asked, "May I work as a flight attendant to pay for my trip?" She was allowed to fly without having to work. When Mother Teresa traveled by train, she always sat in the lower class section. In India she had a free pass for the railways and for the airlines. During the tedious hours of travel and of walking, she and her sisters prayed, especially the rosary.

Mother Teresa opened homes in the United States. In New York her sisters began working with disadvantaged African American communities and fighting racism. They soon spread to other cities: Chicago, San Francisco, Washington, D.C. Today they have many houses throughout the United States.

Finally in 1978, Mother Teresa was able to open a home in Yugoslavia, which was a socialist state. Four sisters moved into a small house behind the cathedral in Zagreb.

By this time Mother Teresa could no longer speak her native Albanian language. She had forgotten it.

Once again, Mother Teresa visited her hometown of Skopje and her father's grave. In speaking to the people there she said, "There is so much poverty here as well. Did you know? Do you know and love the poor? If you do not know them, how can you love them? Well, start in your own homes. In your own families, at home, start there, and God will help you."

To Mother Teresa all of her sisters were like family. She knew each one and kept in touch with the houses worldwide. Often she would be up past midnight writing letters and praying. When someone asked, "Don't you need more sleep?" she would reply with a twinkle in her eye, "There will be time enough for that in the next world!"

Mother Teresa was pleased when other people were inspired by her example of service to the poor. Wealthy people and poor, young and old joined in her work. One day a beggar came to the convent asking for her. He held a metal bowl with his day's earnings. When Mother appeared, he said, "Here. This is for you." Mother Teresa knew that he probably wouldn't eat that night, but she accepted his gift.

Heads of governments and religious leaders were influenced by Mother Teresa too. Many of them visited her or invited her to visit them. She always wore her simple sari, sandals, and no stockings. Sometimes she also used a black cardigan sweater. After President Reagan had met with Mother Teresa for an hour, a reporter asked, "What did you say to her?" The president answered, "When you are with Mother Teresa, you listen!"

19

GRATITUDE AND HONORS

Mother Teresa received her first public award in 1962. The President of India presented her with the Prize of the Miraculous Lotus. She was the first foreigner to receive this prize. Soon after she got home, Mother Teresa hung the medal on the statue of the Blessed Virgin in her Home for the Dying.

That same year a sister called from Agra and said, "Mother, I need 50,000 rupees. There's an urgent need to start a house for the children here."

Mother Teresa replied, "That is too much, my daughter. I will call you back. For the moment we have nothing."

The phone rang again.

"Mother Teresa? This is an editor from the press agency. The Philippine government has just awarded you the Magsaysay Prize. Heartfelt congratulations! It involves a considerable sum of money."

"Thank you for letting me know," Mother responded.

"What do you plan to do with the 50,000 rupees from the prize?"

"Did you say 50,000 rupees?" asked Mother. "I plan to build a home for children at Agra!"

In 1971 Pope Paul VI awarded Mother Teresa the Pope John XXIII Peace Prize. In the same year she received the Good Samaritan award in Boston as well as the John F. Kennedy International Award in Washington. The University of Washington awarded her an honorary doctorate in sociology for demonstrating how solutions can be found for social problems. This was the first of the many honorary doctorates she would receive.

Then in 1973 Mother Teresa became the first recipient of the Templeton Award for Progress in Religion. During her acceptance speech in London she said, "And if we look round we will see many [poor], not as many as in Calcutta, not as many maybe as in other places, but here there are many. Even if it is one, he is Jesus, he is the one that is hungry for love, for care."

Two years later, in 1975, Mother Teresa won The Albert Schweitzer International Prize. Her portrait also appeared on the cover of *Time* Magazine.

The most significant prize of all came to Mother Teresa in 1979. She was chosen as the recipient of the world-renowned Nobel Peace Prize. Her first response was, "I am unworthy." Then she said, "I will accept it on behalf of the poor." Newspapers and magazines all over the globe sang her praises. In Bangalore, the *Deccon Herald* wrote, "Mother Teresa has become a living saint, a legend even during her lifetime, because she has dedicated her all to the service of the most miserable, to those who most need understanding and love."

Receiving the Nobel Peace Prize was for Mother Teresa another opportunity to promote Gospel values. She asked that the traditional banquet not be held. The committee complied and gave her the money saved instead. She used it to feed 2,000 poor people on Christmas Day!

The Nobel Prize was presented to Mother Teresa in Oslo, Norway. The tiny nun landed at the airport in freezing weather, wearing sandals and carrying a simple bag. On the night of the award, she stood at the podium, a slight figure wrapped in a white sari of coarse cotton, which cost about one dollar. Before her was an impressive assembly which included her brother Lazar, Ann

Blaikie, Jacqueline de Decker, and her first two postulants, Sister Agnes and Sister Gertrude. Mother began by making the sign of the cross on her lips as she always did before giving a speech. She invited the 800 people present to pray St. Francis of Assisi's prayer for peace. Then for an hour, without notes, she spoke of the need for peace and love and of the world's problems, such as abortion.

With the eyes of the world upon her, Mother Teresa told of her works and of people who had sacrificed to help the poor. She also exhorted her audience: "There is so much suffering, so much hate, so much misery; to remedy this we must start in our homes with prayers and sacrifices. Love is born in homes."

She went on, "I want you to try to look for the poor, first in your own house, and there begin with love. Be the good news for your loved ones. Take interest in your neighbors. Do you know who your neighbors are?"

She encouraged, "Let us do the essential: that not one single child may be unwanted, that we may meet each other and smile, especially when it is hard to smile."

The publicity surrounding the Nobel Prize was an ordeal for the humble Mother Teresa. Photographers and reporters hounded her. When she returned to the motherhouse, word spread through the halls, "Mother's home!" The excited sisters gathered at the entrance. Mother Teresa was soon swamped by a sea of white saris. One sister asked, "How does it feel to be famous?" Mother exclaimed, "For that publicity alone, I should go straight to heaven!"

When Mother Teresa returned to India, the government prepared a great banquet to celebrate her award. Mother Teresa refused to come, saying, "I could not take part and eat all that food with a clear conscience, knowing how many of my brothers and sisters even today are dying of hunger." Other guests also refused to come, and the banquet was cancelled. The food was taken to Nirmal Hriday. To Mother's delight, government officials and other important guests went there and fed the people.

In 1980 Mother Teresa was honored with the most prestigious award of India: the Bharat Ratna—Jewel of India. In 1983 Queen Elizabeth conferred on her the highest award given by the British government, reception into the Order of Merit. Two years later, in 1985, President Reagan presented her with the Medal of Freedom, the highest civilian honor of the United States. In 1997 she also received the United States Congressional Medal of Honor.

Throughout all of this attention, Mother Teresa remained simple, poor, and unassuming. She valued greater rewards more: a thank you from a dying person, peace, and the joy that comes from being close to God.

20

COURAGEOUS LOVE

Mother Teresa and her sisters went where other people feared to go. They ventured into leper colonies, AIDS hospitals, and hospices. When disaster struck a country—cyclones, floods, earthquakes, or human-made violence—Mother Teresa's Missionaries of Charity were often among the first to respond.

When Mother heard of the civil war in Ireland, she sent sisters to open a house in Belfast to support the widows and orphans. Unfortunately, they were not welcome there and had to leave. Mother Teresa's response to any failure was, "We are called upon not to be successful but to be faithful."

In 1981 Ethiopia experienced a great famine. Mother Teresa brought medicine and food from Calcutta. It wasn't enough. Neither was the help offered by the relief agencies because the distribution was unorganized. Mother Teresa sent a telegram to President Reagan of the United States asking for aid. He called her and promised to help. Food arrived soon, and it was delivered to where it was really needed.

Mother Teresa arrived in Beirut, Lebanon in 1982 at the peak of the conflict there. In West Beirut, where the fighting was the fiercest, thirty-seven mentally ill children were trapped without food or water. When Mother heard this, she volunteered to rescue them. "That's like committing suicide!" one man exclaimed. Nevertheless Mother and her sisters rode in a Red Cross van to rescue the children. The snipers held their fire.

In 1985 Mother Teresa opened the first Catholic Church-sponsored home in New York City for people with AIDS.

A devastating earthquake in Armenia in 1988 gave her an opening into the communist Soviet Union. Soon she had founded ten houses within that country. She called her houses "tabernacles," or houses of God.

A friend once remarked to Mother, "You're the most powerful woman in the world!"

With a smile, Mother Teresa replied, "I wish I was. Then I would bring peace to the whole world."

In many ways Mother Teresa resembled her hero, Mahatma Gandhi, who had led the peaceful struggle to gain India's independence. Gandhi had focused on basic values such as peace and compassion, especially through his use of nonviolent means.

In 1991 when the United States and Iraq were locked in conflict, Mother Teresa wrote to President George Bush and Saddam Hussein, pleading for peace. Afterwards she received a letter from Hussein in which he invited her sisters to Iraq to help with the orphaned and disabled. They accepted the invitation.

That same year a cyclone devastated the coastal cities of Bangladesh. An estimated 300,000 people died. Mother Teresa had just been discharged from the hospital where she had been treated for a heart problem. Immediately she and two sisters took boxes of medicine and flew in a helicopter to visit the survivors. They were accompanied by the Prime Minister of Bangladesh. Mother's presence there, which was broadcast on television, led others to come forward and help.

Some people criticized Mother Teresa because she dealt directly with the poor instead of getting involved with politics and trying to eliminate the causes of poverty. She would explain, "My concern is poor, suffering people and their needs. Others can focus on why they are poor."

How did Mother and her sisters find the strength and courage to do their challenging work? They did it all for Jesus. Their love for him spurred them on.

They did everything *for Jesus and found strength in him.*

21

FINAL SUFFERINGS

Mother Teresa had never enjoyed good health. Near the end of her life she suffered from heart problems. These first occurred in 1983 while she was visiting Pope John Paul II in Rome.

In 1989 Mother Teresa suffered another heart attack, which was almost fatal. She underwent surgery and had a pacemaker implanted. The following year she intended to resign as the head of her community of sisters. She got permission from Rome to hold an election a year early. The community was to choose her successor by secret ballot. When the ballots were counted, all votes were for her except one—her own!

During a visit to Mexico in 1991, Mother Teresa came down with pneumonia, which led to heart failure. This time she was hospitalized in La Jolla, California. When she had a relapse in Rome, Princess Diana of England, who shared her love for the poor, made a special trip to visit her there. The young blond princess and the nun with the wrinkled, weather-beaten face became friends.

While in Rome in May of 1993, Mother Teresa fell and broke three ribs. She came down with malaria that August. This was followed by surgery to clear a blocked blood vessel.

Mother Teresa fell again in 1996. This time she broke her collarbone. She also battled malaria, a chest infection, and underwent heart surgery. During that same year she became an honorary citizen of the United States. She was only the fourth person to ever receive this honor.

Not until March 13, 1997 did Mother Teresa formally step down from the top leadership role in her community. Sister Nirmala, leader of the contemplative branch of the Missionaries of Charity, was chosen to be head of the community. She said, "I will not be called Mother. We have only one Mother."

A few months later, on September 5, 1997, Mother Teresa did some bookkeeping for her community's institutions. Then she made arrangements to attend a memorial for Princess Diana, her friend, whose funeral had taken place the week before. Suddenly at 9:00 P.M. Mother Teresa called,

"Sister, I feel faint." She collapsed, unconscious, onto her bed. A doctor was summoned, but there was nothing he could do. Mother Teresa died at 9:32 that night. She was eighty-seven years old. The strong hands that had caressed so many babies, that had gently cleaned the wounds of so many sick and had prayed so many rosaries, were still.

As Jacques Chirac, the French Prime Minister, declared at the time, "Tonight there's less love, less compassion, less light in the world."

Mother Teresa has gone to be with the Lord whom she loved so much, but she has left behind an extraordinary legacy. Her more than 4,000 Sisters, 400 priests and brothers, and at least 100,000 Co-workers continue to show love in action throughout the world. They continue to follow the way that Mother Teresa described on her "business card":

THE SIMPLE PATH
The fruit of silence is PRAYER.
The fruit of prayer is FAITH.
The fruit of faith is LOVE.
The fruit of love is SERVICE.
The fruit of service is PEACE.

22

"Saint" of the People

The young Indian boy faced the reporter and boasted, "I've come here every day!" He was standing in rain in 95-degree weather outside of St. Thomas Church, where Mother Teresa was waked for almost a week. Every day some 50,000 people of all faiths came to pay their respects.

Mother Teresa's funeral was held on September 10, 1997—the anniversary of her "second call" fifty-one years earlier. Her funeral was impressive. Her white casket was borne in a gun carriage that had last been used to carry the body of Mahatma Gandhi. Her coffin was given a military escort as it wound its way through the streets of Calcutta, and she was honored with a 21-gun salute.

The funeral for the woman called "the saint of the gutters" was held in the Netaji Indian Stadium, which seats 12,000. Many dignitaries were present, including a representative of Pope John Paul II. Sister Nirmala insisted that some seats be reserved for the poor. Mother Teresa's open casket was draped with an Indian flag. She had become an Indian citizen in 1948. The altar behind the casket bore a banner which read "Works of love are works of peace." During the offertory of the Mass, Sister Nirmala brought up a pencil, in memory of Mother Teresa's words, "I am a pencil in God's hands. God writes through us, and however imperfect we may be, he writes beautifully."

Afterwards Mother Teresa's body was taken back to the motherhouse. There in her home she was buried. The marker at her grave reads, "Love one another as I have loved you." A wall of the convent was opened onto the street so that people could visit her grave.

People all over the world expected that Mother Teresa would not have to wait long to be canonized, that is, be officially declared a saint. And they were right. Ordinarily there is a five-year waiting period before the process begins. But Pope John Paul II waived this for Mother Teresa. The investigation into the holiness of her life began less than two years after her death.

Before someone is beatified, a step towards canonization, a miracle must be worked. A non-Christian Indian woman named Monica Besra received a miracle through Mother Teresa's intercession. Mrs. Besra, the mother of five children, had a large tumor in her stomach. The Missionaries of Charity prayed to Mother Teresa for her and placed a medal that bore her image on the woman's stomach. On the first anniversary of Mother Teresa's death, Mrs. Besra woke to discover that the large tumor had disappeared! The Pope accepted this cure as the required miracle. On October 19, 2003, the Church proclaimed Mother Teresa of Calcutta "Blessed." This means that she is now just one step away from being named a saint.

Navin Chawla, a biographer of Mother Teresa, wrote what most people thought: "She's our foremost conscience-keeper. The world has already anointed her a saint. Anything that comes along from the Church in five or fifty years is just a formality."

The Missionaries of Charity continue to carry on Mother Teresa's spirit and work. During the 2003 attacks on Iraq when others chose to evacuate the country, her sisters at the orphanage stayed. Today Mother Teresa's family of religious staff 697 centers for the poor in 131 countries! Following in her footsteps—feeding the hungry, giving drink to the thirsty, welcoming the stranger, clothing the naked, visiting the ill and imprisoned—they find Jesus in the poorest of the poor, for Jesus has promised, "Whatever you did for one of these least ones, you did for me" (Matthew 25:40).

PRAYER

Blessed Teresa of Calcutta, you bravely answered God's call twice and taught the world how to put love into action. You saw Jesus in the poorest of the poor and responded with love. The dying, unwanted children, the lepers and the abandoned all came to know God's love through you.

Now pray for us, that we too may answer God's call to do more. Let us trust God to provide for us as we do what he wants. May we follow your advice to love until it hurts and do it with a smile, beginning with our family and friends. Then we too will make our lives something beautiful for God! Amen.

Glossary

1. **Brother**—a male religious who makes vows of poverty, chastity, and obedience and lives in community.

2. **Canonization**—the Church's official declaration that a person has lived a life of heroic virtue and is in heaven.

3. **Constitutions**—a religious congregation's rule of life that explains its spirit and purpose and gives guidelines for the members. Constitutions are approved by Church officials in Rome.

4. **Contemplative**—describes a community whose members focus on prayer and union with God as opposed to an active community with ministries outside of the convent.

5. **Exclaustration**—a situation in which a religious sister, brother or priest lives apart from the community for a certain time.

6. **Habit**—the clothing that identifies a religious as a member of a community.

7. **Intercession**—a type of prayer in which God's help is asked. Jesus **intercedes**

for us with God the Father. The Blessed Mother and the saints also intercede with God on our behalf.

8. **Mission**—(as used in this book) a central location from which a priest and his helpers would not only bring the message of Jesus to the people of a certain area for the first time, but also minister to their needs. While always including a chapel or church for the celebration of Mass, a mission could also include a school or clinic.

9. **Motherhouse**—the main building and headquarters of a religious community.

10. **Novena**—a prayer prayed for nine days, hours, or months.

11. **Novice**—a person being formed as a religious. A novice may wear the habit and have a religious name, but he or she hasn't made vows.

12. **Pilgrimage**—a journey to a holy place to honor God.

13. **Postulant**—a person taking first steps in religious life; a candidate.

14. **Poverty**—as a vow, giving up material goods for the sake of being closer to God.

15. **Retreat**—a period of prayer and silence for renewing one's spiritual life.

16. **Rosary**—a prayer in which we think about events in the lives of Jesus and Mary while saying Our Fathers, Hail Marys and Glory Bes on a circle of beads.

17. **Sacrifice**—a gift offered to God, such as something difficult that we do.

18. **Sodality**—an organization dedicated to Mary in which people deepen their prayer life and perform works of charity.

19. **Spiritual director**—one who guides a person in the Christian life.

20. **Superior**—in a religious congregation the leader of a house or the community.

21. **Vocation**—a call from God to a lifestyle, such as the married life, single life, priesthood or religious life. Everyone has a vocation to be holy.

22. **Vow**—a solemn promise made to God. Religious priests, brothers and sisters usually make vows of poverty, chastity, and obedience.

BOOKS & MEDIA

The Daughters of St. Paul operate book and media centers at the following addresses. Visit, call or write the one nearest you today, or find us on the World Wide Web, www.pauline.org

CALIFORNIA
3908 Sepulveda Blvd, Culver City, CA 90230 — 310-397-8676
5945 Balboa Avenue, San Diego, CA 92111 — 858-565-9181
2650 Broadway Street, Redwood City, CA 94063

FLORIDA
145 S.W. 107th Avenue, Miami, FL 33174 — 305-559-6715

HAWAII
1143 Bishop Street, Honolulu, HI 96813 — 808-521-2731
Neighbor Islands call: — 800-259-8463

ILLINOIS
172 North Michigan Avenue, Chicago, IL 60601 — 312-346-4228

LOUISIANA
4403 Veterans Memorial Blvd, Metairie, LA 70006 — 504-887-7631

MASSACHUSETTS
885 Providence Hwy, Dedham, MA 02026 — 781-326-5385

MISSOURI
9804 Watson Road, St. Louis, MO 63126 — 314-965-3512

NEW JERSEY
561 U.S. Route 1, Wick Plaza, Edison, NJ 08817 — 732-572-1200

NEW YORK
150 East 52nd Street, New York, NY 10022 — 212-754-1110

PENNSYLVANIA
9171-A Roosevelt Blvd, Philadelphia, PA 19114 — 215-676-9494

SOUTH CAROLINA
243 King Street, Charleston, SC 29401 — 843-577-0175

TENNESSEE
4811 Poplar Avenue, Memphis, TN 38117 — 901-761-2987

TEXAS
114 Main Plaza, San Antonio, TX 78205 — 210-224-8101

VIRGINIA
1025 King Street, Alexandria, VA 22314 — 703-549-3806

CANADA
3022 Dufferin Street, Toronto, ON M6B 3T5 — 416-781-9131